TO ABEL AND OTHERS

Patrick
CREAGH

THE BODLEY HEAD
LONDON SYDNEY
TORONTO

ISBN 0 370 01337 9
Printed and bound in Great Britain for
The Bodley Head Ltd
9 Bow Street, London, WC2
by William Clowes and Sons Ltd, Beccles
Set in Monotype Bembo
First published 1970

TO ABEL AND OTHERS

BY THE SAME AUTHOR

A Row of Pharaohs

A Picture of Tristan: Imitations of Tristan Corbière

Dragon Jack-knifed

CONTENTS

TO ABEL
DAY BY DAY

AUTHOR'S NOTE

I ask the reader to bear in mind that the speaker is always Cain, that 'you' is always Abel, and that if Abel is never referred to as Cain's 'brother' this is for a good reason.

* I was running and running till rust
was in the mouth the chest
forced acetylene I was finished

Sharp as in grass the cars
hissing at corners
lights
        all night they'd cleave the ceiling
        and my small bed unsafe
sickle the last dark yards
sweet smell of harvest
blood
        my dog once at mowing that got among
                                                            the men
        its foot cut off

The last stalk
I wait
am caught

I prayed then for tall grass for trees
green under green under green for a well a wall
for underbrush where no light comes
for places we called secret for secrets
made up to please us when there was no need
Abel I prayed

and ran

bent on a kerb against a
wrenching wind between a
sea so far below no sound of its
wolfpacks its green vipers
climbed

and a suburban pavement
grey   slab   traps
heavily too heavily each
footfall fearing a manhole
under which?

Under which are doctor and priest
expecting their cold office?

I was running and running till
at the corner
bolas of lights
            it roared in air it dazzled
brought me down

* Palms on wet stone
stench of black rain

It got among the men

But no one came
no one took aim

Shutters closed blinds down
latticed the empty Underground

And so until the first black
bulk of brick
diluted to dead grey
first bus cold and empty-handed
outside an all-night café
three negroes do not notice me

Only you now
beloved Abel

* To places known

In grief
always the same
the safe way back

The familiar street
so many mellowed words
the only comfort a cliché

* I found the old house and it was empty
but each room a nursery
now I am missing your voice
in the cellars where we hid from bedtime

The furniture has gone somewhere
the old trunks have vanished
there is nothing under dustsheets
I am missing your voice

On bare stone my foot
strikes echoes from beyond
silence and my shoes leave
no mark in the level dust

There is nothing to remember

* Abel beyond silence
and beyond the crumbling
undiscovered limits of fatigue

I went deeper
fumbled on endless steps

always a colder tunnel
always a narrower seam

In veins of fire and ore
I moved and was bruised till
into the narrowest cleft
cheek laid in the rock's saliva

rest

* There was nothing to remember
but there was a light
paining from above revealing
in the frailty of an eyelid
the grip of thirsting roots

Skull a tender membrane
bubble of blood and water
frailty of an eyelid
veins burning in darker knots
a mesh of branding wires

Waking and taken
red into daylight
barked on barbed roots
till the sun pricks above me in a
mesh of binding wires

Ore drawn from a narrow mine
heavily too heavily
I stand in the stubble

Is there nothing to remember?
What was the act we shared?

It was summer I had flayed
the last sheaf

And then?

* You lie in the stubble, naked, your white arms useless, as they were always useless, your hands turned up as if waiting for rain, as you were always waiting

your head turned as if watching a bird perch on your shoulder, and so they would perch, often, you were so still, always so quiet and still

and your belly a bowl of milk and the great wound between your legs and blood among the stubble

* Outcries for love and anguish

From your red groin grows the tree
heavy already with scarlet berries

Moon-ripened in their
almost skinless eagerness

Their seeds turn parasite

* What ailed you world-weary Abel
always so quiet and still

Useless among knotted roots
you lie where you were broken

I chose I stood up I took weapon
the air sang it fire began it
heretic I
chose

You dawdled a small while then
idled a longer and
what enthralled?

You saw but looked not
heard not listened
mantled in a dream that played
always the same green note

Light was golden
dripped from trees
as I set out

* Hardened as day grew round

I looked over my shoulder
almost the full strength of noon
ring of fire almost perfectly
turned and tuned

You had diluted to a pool
mere gift of rain

I went on

* For I dreamt a city

A planned landscape

trellis and terrace
cypress to mark a boundary
hedges and bridges
roads to places

* I went on

Rounding to noon
pain turned to pride

Iron guilt
not milk forgiveness

Breath of fire
not
liquefaction of a prayer

Not fitful torrent hope
not uneasy dream of sea

From the uneasy dream
time deliver me

* What ailed you world-weary Abel
useless among knotted roots

I throw you down look I am taller
a paved road answers shod feet
a city throws aurora on
otherwise night

I throw you down my fingers seize
tongs from the fire my lens cuts down

eternity to proper size
these flashing atoms are my own

I throw you down I raise you up
to wring some music from your lip
I cage you to assuage my need
I tend your parasitic seed

Where I will you
stand or run
I create you time and again
only to kill you

For I am a man

* Not peace but a sword

thus

I brought to light

* Bone upon bone
buried

Stone upon stone
built

Shod feet upon paving

Sunlight opens the shutters
a new day like a new book
study it
write out tomorrow

At the cross of four ways
the great tree grows
in its shade a patient murmur
old men gathering at evening
hang it with leaves

Heart of the city
blood at the root

Gentleness did not exist
until I killed it

* What shall I tell my son?

Say no
rip the unwanted gift
conceive at dawn
achieve at noon
make shade obey
exactitude
cast by the straightness of your line

Make space obey

Time and again called up
time and again thrown down

O clay

* I turn to you late
advise me

What can your death tell me
of what grows bright with blood

papaver somniferum

O let me sleep

* I stand by the pool

under the sun a blue eye
at night a silver mirror

Animals come to the pool
drink and are satisfied

Unobserved and negligent
water fills their footprints

I alone look in the pool
under the sun a staring eye
at night a willing mirror

and see myself

White upright soft and bare
but for a dark blur called pudendum
feet tender among the stubble
and I lack tooth and claw

I am unsatisfied

* So much the rather

* I left no footprint in the mud
but a paved way
in adamant to last for ever

At windows and doorways
my apprehensive brethren crouched
binding their genitals in rags
guarding the soft parts of their bellies

Lest they should kill me
I bore the note of infamy

Later we called it law

For I was the first to cut
into that easy pasture
into the green of dreams
first to see
red earth smoulder under grass
to quicken it
to break it and make it
mine

* For I dreamt a city
four-square
impregnable
under the sun a garden of voices
at night a square of light set fast in space

For the heart cannot live on the hill
for the dark is always more enormous
for what we cannot fathom we must fear
for the sheep are nothing to go by
for I bore the mark of infamy

for we must abide by one another
for there is always strength and greed
for the weak and meek are the greater number
for what we fear we must work to know
for what we know we master

For I had dreamt a paradox
a land sacred to reason
sea rock temple golden section
honeycomb
                    gods of geometry
And so it was but

* My stacks fume under the horizon
summer is over them
heavy indifferent
her breasts are milkless but
their dry soft haloes mock
my stacks upright under the horizon
always new
dying that is
under the horizon

My vapours shift
but your escarpment stays
heavy indifferent

Summer now winter soon
and your humiliating favours
your watershed your cold excess
gifts I cannot resist
stored in your paralysing snows
my fields swell your hips regale them
my fruit awaits your parting thighs

Yet I was the first to cut
into that milk of infancy
I made you work to cool my burns

My stacks fume under the horizon
under your dead escarpment

Always under your horizon
I fume I make I waste

Staggered at the half-life of love
barely a breathing space

* No sun

Lid of aluminum

I in my corner of the courtyard the mist thickens
no face utters its anguish at the window only
the fountain drops grief in a green bowl
inconsólable incónsolable where you have fallen
Abel and I am gathering to the fall
and my son gathers too young to talk gathers

Mist thickens no sign of the sun no finger
pointing of sun and shade soon I am lost
and you are the nearer for that
lost
your burial always under my feet today
hollow on cobbles you hear them do you
inconsólable incónsolable
always nearing always going away

The wall between us thin last night
thin as an eyelid I could hear your failure

One grain does not make a heap nor two
nor three
then when does the heap begin
One day
one day does not make a death
nevertheless

Timeless formless inconsolable

Lid of aluminum

No sun

* Evening and
stillness of wings

White upright soft and bare
I am alone with night things

Turning and turning
at each turn I find
warm nest and swart fear
net the mind

* Waste of separation I
nothing mine
nothing I

taste of absence

* What is your life
divided? My
keen drill finds no
sign of you

Hazel twig with
not a shock in
hand is dry

* The city runs
crossing to crossing
torn with wind

Round each corner the same man's
body lies

I don't want to look
but my head's pushed down

Face changes as wind changes
but the clothes are mine

* Your tacit spells
bound me

I am without them
my own invention

I

* God how the wind tears at the tiles
sounding the emptinesses of the house
in which
I sit
so alone the house forgets me

* Abel ambiguous ghost
always so quiet and still
now you surround me with
green stakes driven in

that take root and spread
a hedge of prickly-pear
languor of succulents
that flower unexpectedly

Sweetness within
a husk untouchable
with sweet and silently
you shut me in

* Yet under grass in tall green
in damp places
rumours of you

Where no sun

The grass whispers kinship
and the reeds
hint at an understanding

I am heavy I tread them down

* But the dark is always more enormous
mindless confineless

It creeps in easily at sleeping windows

* Makes dreams where I had thought
was only rest

You alone with your kind
in a level place
me also alone a fallen husk
the wrong side of sunset

I don't want to look
there is a screen of leaves
easily I could flee to hard
cover of rock

but I am forced with longing

* I visited your secret grove
only the full moon for light
and the reflecting stream

Women who seemed beams of moonlight
oiled your whitest limbs your breasts
your belly gleamed a pool of silver
light indulgent hands caressed
your slackening flanks and tender labia

Your body broke the moon still shines
on the urgency of water

that mocks in its broken mirror
the dark longing of the pines

O rites of exile

* I ran as dreaming
sex
weighing me down

black under black under
black and backlash
of twigs unseen until it bled
white into dawn

And crawl weighed down
into the forge of noon

Remade a man

* A narrow door
a spiral
stair

O rites

At top of it
a skylight like a pearl

O rites

I tread steps down
with every breath I lose
some definition of the flesh

In the room faintlighted I
watch you undress
proffer your body like a bowl

All day long a tender eye
at night a willing mirror

I see the red earth under grass
quicken it
break it and make it
mine
your white arms useless

In the same room at the same root
our love and hate

O rites

From your red groin grows the tree
heavy already with scented berries

* Moon-ripened in their
almost skinless eagerness

Their seeds turn parasite

Acetylene flames
tore at the skin's seams

* Dark blur upon
the white limbs of my pilgrimage

Ineradicable stain
on my almost perfected flesh

Aceldema where I return
time and again
rooted in desire to burst
into a crime
that is an image of the first

* Gold iron fire air
hammer and
ploughshare

mind music and machine
melt in the lapping of your dream

room warm clad shod
invention founders in your mud

dead sun sheds you on horizon
great moon tugs your tides of blood

viscous sister in whose slime
I sleep the sleep of earth

and blood

* Brute menstrual stench I curse your
dribbling abortions
terrible warm dreams

Viscous sister in whose slime
I sleep the sleep of blood and love

Tender O tender
longings hurling
son upon son to murder and hunger

I am sick of men and their sons and their
sons' sons
their blunders and their sons' blunders
their grins and their guns

For I had dreamt a paradox
a land sacred to reason
and so it was
but for a dark blur called pudendum
but for time
dripping slow
but for you in tall green
but for you O willing mirror
but for the waves

* How I have fought you
fought your death
not to die it

To become fire
never to deliquesce
To be
Heraclitean energy

Your love a sleep I woke from that
contained a dream that tainted me
tepid milk of infancy

douce poison that
from my lip
I spit

* Turn to the pool
never

never look in that blank eye
never that willing mirror

on the dead beach of dream
never set footprint

Humid ghost
hung on my right arm
your creeping lowliness
betrayed the upright man

I throw you down

useless

* Tongs from the fire with you
in this first instant
of unmoted light
I consecrate this house a pyre
hearth where dreamers sat
table where the lies went round
let dead books no more enclose
their static message
let skeletal
rafters crack
their glowing barbs
pierce the heart
of the vampire hidden since I was a child
under the stairs among the bric-à-brac

I walk out clean
white and upright

hard as formica
shrivel the false green of trees
the silly hopes of grass burn up

* Bone upon bone
built

I chose I stood up I took weapon
air sang it fire began it
my craftsman's hands
crooked to the haft

Upright
by an act
that dogs me

I dreamt a city
stone upon stone

buried

* Square of light set fast in space

O wake
to a stone logic

Hands crooked to the haft

* Running and running
rust
burning acetylene
no hopes of grass to cool my feet

Somewhere the shrinking ocean but

Full strength of noon
in whose fist I
fall
inert
rawbacked on burning sand

O Abel earth's last tree is ash

* Air sang it fire began it
all the windows of the world returned to tears

that people looked through
figuring a dream in
tall green

Come with your tide
cool my burns

I am afraid of your last depths
fish in their own monstrous light

otherwise night

Gift of rain
cool my burns
monstrous ineradicable waves

Only you now
cruel Abel
you can drown me I can let you

Nevertheless

SMALL PICTURE OF YOU IN A PROSPECT OF FLOWERS

I

To find tenderness, catch him, have a good look at him,
hard thing, for he is softly and in
secret, seemingly nowhere

It is no good in the woods
still less on cobbles, calling his name
but he is always there, sprightly alight
a pilot flame

He is impish at heart, careless
knowing he holds in his seedling palm the whole
cool green growth of happiness

as now and today, driving south
shows me your body in every valley
and little things of spring speak out
some green words from your mouth

This is their time to rival you
whom all this spring from Rome to Spanda
imitates
celebrates

while there at home both fig and vine
put honeybuds out
fumble all-thumbs

and you in the morning, hair in tendrils
numbly rub at sticky small
half opened dreams

2

Time in the end
will not suffer us
so while the season is we'd better spit
cherrystones into his hatbrim as he
portly passes beneath our window

3

I write not to pull
a flash of silver
from an indifferent pool

to plead shriek mercy trap attention
give pity root
offer as benison
myself
or shackle you with love

but to describe you
hoping I may surprise you
in your bodily solitude
and make things around you listen
as I do
for breath and step
and all your rhythms

4

A landscape
wholly laden

valley between low hills
that opens like an apricot or
afternoon

there is heat in it
as in the palm of a hand
holding a coin

at its foot a
sea-lough a salt inlet

Here in old times
adventurous men ran in
their long ships swilling with silver

but I have stayed here
savoured and suffered
all your seasons
your tide has stranded me
and carried me
I've swum under the lion sun
alone
searched your salt bed
strewn with wrecks
and surfaced
reluctantly
laden with gold moidores

5

and in the spiral
spiralling
until walls run
with liquid pearl

and we like gliding
ghosts pass
into our effigies
and sleep

6

A long road, easy to lose

Deep woods, dragon shadows
no one before me dared them

A convent in the mountains where
nuns bend to their mysteries
at midnight with muffled candles

No honey or sunshine
here, no deciduous leaf
but yew and cypress, trees
dark green with grief

No berries, strawberries
no dripping figs, no pool
but a deep well waterless
nothing to flow or grow
but black bitter olives
that ripen in December snow

Skin tough, resistant
it takes a stone to make
heavy oil of that dark flesh
as now erect in prayer between
snow-whitened hills the hard
ritual black figures press
into their narrow mysteries

Long time, and trial
great stones churning prayer to oil
swelling song forbidden words

till a flash of silver white
sweet reply
scored into their moonless night

7

Six hours ago
your breasts were two
fresh cones thrown up
a film restraining
molten cores

and now on milk
of morning hang
as on a cheek two
perfect tears

8

You and morning side by side
the two new things
stand at the window

You stretch and the young sun
also

and I write a few lines
hoping they might resemble you
standing on tiptoe

9

The moon also
fondles you
but I fear not her
viscous kisses

nor her steely unrequited
instruments

She sips at your coral
chalice her tongue's mercurial
her rites are ancient but
her prayers
are breathed
into a tabernacle scented but empty

While this
morning is
upstart Apollo is
randy is rival he
ripens you pale into gold

and you turn away from me
to catch your breath
at reckless day

10

Lie still lest I dare
stand up a champion

and even so
body distended so
one thigh asleep upon the other
head on hand
green eyes flecked with brown
watching
such cool and carelessness
and yet

a hip
        to tempt a waterfall

a waist
        to fling a noose

11

Yet at times
seeming alight only because
light encircles you

a lake under a windless
winter sun

a still
cold
sapphire

12

Fall of a breast
intent and serious

aureoles pupils of your soul
dilate before the gaze of day

O if a god looked in he would not
turn unsatisfied away

so do not stray too far towards
the perihelion of June
lest you should turn and see
your body burnt
reflected in his breastplate
noon

13

Again you stand
framed in candid windowpanes
while beyond
the new leaves also open
little by little

14

You knocked up a new dress
in less time than it takes me
to write down this

and when you came in
suddenly wearing it
I was
dumb

at the river in you
that I never kiss
the same face twice

springs I cannot trace
falls I do not dare
cities traffic navigation
estuary of unsighted shores

while I am the same stone
set and involuntary
hardly aware of your
patient
shock of attrition

15

What I might have meant to say
concerning you
will be hidden to the last

as a movement you make
twist or turn or sudden grace
remains hidden
in the air when you have passed

CRITICAL APPARATUS

1

How can I write in straight lines
when all my thoughts are
bound Sebastians
bristling with paradox?

Every poem starts
at the heart of a cross
and then bleeds white
at all extremes.

Nailed hand and foot
I march to freedom
but am tied down
by rootlessness.

I might hope, but.
I'd even pray, if.
I long for a thing
perfectly singular.

Not this cowering heroism
not this couchant stance
not this fiendish joy
not this dismembered dance.

2

How can I close the circle
of a well-turned world
when every spree
fires off a tangent
new incongruity?

3

My resolutions fall, dead leaves
cover the ground no thicker.
So many items to forget to write
in the little diary I never got round to buying.

4

Take a mute thought
bend it
till it catches light

Blow upon this
redden it and
hammer

Let it cool

Consider

5

Here I go again
'decorating the obvious with wholesome
imagery'
as some
clever lowbrow critic wrote
(under a pseudonym).

Well, poor boy,
I have exchanged formalities with Cerberus
and that's going far enough.

Let him take on where I left off.

6

I am six foot four but light boned
voice scarcely a whisper
my word upon the page weighs
little

But there it is

I invite you Maevius to consider me
your opposite

7

One of these days Maevius
you'll find your hair receding
your mirror smile and glow at you
so pleased to see
the welcoming space above your eyebrows

And the guests will gather
in the weeded forecourt
and you will be shy at first
after so long in mourning
for your long dead hopes

8

I could name you some poets
who'll write you a greasy pole
out of a plain old wooden shaft
(don't worry, it's not far to fall)

while I cross-hatch the handle
to let you get a grip on me

and write to you in words of
mendacious simplicity

9

How long the abandoned garden

For creepers and dreamers
neglect intensifies

But all stalk and no flowers
sooner or later the watcher tires
the clock runs down in the summerhouse

A look over the wall would show
longingly familiar streets
the bars bloom out these summer nights
the talk goes round

In the abandoned garden
no sound

Stay poet though
stay that unheard-of thing

to be

LEAST WILL AND TESTAMENT

The prisoner at the bar asserts

that poetry is a republic based on nothing
that as it exists we must give it a seat
among the nations
that its voice is priceless although it has no armies
that it speaks as man to man and brother to brother
that it is the opposite of ideology
that it does not kill or maim for any cause
that it is a cool shade in the desert of living
that it is a beam of light shone upon death
that it is all things to all men and what you will
that critics who limit it must live on crumbs

Strike that from the record

That living is poetry and poetry is my living
that I am congenitally short of cash
that poetry is hard is too hard is impossible
that most who call themselves poets are worse than
I am
that I praise them all the same because they suffer
that I curse them all the same because I suffer
that I believe poetry should be committed
that I commit it every day and am punished for it
that I am thirty-eight and still beginning
that I praise all still beginnings in sounding verse
that whatever I do or say I shall not convince you
that you have bought this book and deserve some
credit
that I write you out a cheque for a thousand thanks
that the bank will not cash it because they are
down to business
that the interest on love is nought per cent
that hard currency can't save a civilization

Strike that from the record

That books are expensive and I can tell you little
that I live as I must in a wine-drinking country
that beer is swill for pigs but wine is a god
that I make him with my own hands and my friends
the enzymes
that I cherish him in cellars cool and dark
that I change his barrel to stop him going musty
that I do this in the last quarter of the moon
that as long as the moon is waning he comes clear
that he grows mellow with age while I decline

That I am married and my son is nearly four
that he has inherited the earth but later will lose it
that I am dull and slow and somewhat lacking
that my wife calls me a fool and I love her for it
that she proves twice one is a hundred and fifty
thousand
that the love of a woman is the beginning of wisdom
that the love of two women is hell's bleeding pincers
that until I was sixteen I believed in God
that now I believe in darkness and light a candle
that this book is a candle I have lit to see by
that some will come with snuffers and put it out
that I have a box of candles and will light another

That I am not afraid of dying but don't want to
that I'd rather be a blade of grass than a dead saint
that living and merely living is infinite variety
that being dead is always the same thing
that the present continuous tense is always with us
that you are my gentle reader and I love you

Strike that from the record

That I cannot see a week into my future
that whatever I do I cannot earn a living
that what I have to give cannot be sold
that I must stop this soon or bore your pants off
that I write this because I have no sense of shame
that I have no sense of shame because I am honest
that I am lost at sea and you are with me
that you are my gentle reader and my companion
that all I can utter may not bring us to landfall
that the shore we long for has yet to be imagined
that the one we know of is cold with no light burning

That I have been to Florence to do some shopping
that I thought up this poem crossing the river
that an unread poem is waste and masturbation
that I ask you gentle reader for your attentions

Strike that from the record

That I am back in the hills and it is summer
that a large bee has landed on the paper
that I am on the road home
that I am glad